Clip-Art Features for Church Newsletters 6

Illustrations for Bulletin Boards,
Home Bulletins, and News Releases

Clip-Art Features for Church Newsletters 6

George W. Knight, Compiler
Howard Paris, Illustrator

BAKER BOOK HOUSE
Grand Rapids, Michigan 49516

Copyright © 1990 by Baker Books
a division of Baker Book House Company
P.O. Box 6287, Grand Rapids, MI 49516-6287

ISBN: 0-8010-5291-2

Third printing, October 1993

Printed in the United States of America

Contents

Introduction

Since the appearance of the first compilation of *Clip-Art Features* in 1984, we have adopted the pattern of producing one new book each year. We are delighted that these short essays and fillers in clip-art format continue to fill a real need in the publishing ministry of thousands of churches.

You can help us keep these books on target with your needs. Let us know how you are using these clip-art items and how they could be made even more useful. Enclose copies of your local church publications in which these clip-art features have appeared. We will consider your suggestions carefully and possibly incorporate them in future clip-art books. The address is Baker Book House, P.O. Box 6287, Grand Rapids, MI 49516.

George W. Knight
Howard Paris

1

Church Attendance and Support

God's "One Another" Plan

The Bible contains a long list of "one anothers." As Christians we should heed especially the following ten "one anothers" in our relationships with our fellow Christians.

1. Love one another (John 13:34).
2. Rejoice with one another (Rom. 12:15).
3. Don't judge one another (Rom. 14:13).
4. Admonish one another (Rom. 15:14).
5. Care for one another (1 Cor. 12:25).
6. Serve one another (Gal. 5:13).
7. Forgive one another (Eph. 4:32).
8. Encourage one another (1 Thess. 5:11).
9. Pray for one another (James 5:16).
10. Bear one another's burdens (Gal. 6:2).

A Singing People

Many books of the Bible include actual hymns or songs. Others refer to occasions which included music or the offering of praise to God. His people have always been a singing people, worshiping him in a spirit of joyous praise.

When we gather for worship, we should heed the words of the psalmist: "It is good to give thanks to the Lord, and sing praises unto thy name, O Most High" (Ps. 92:1).

Backbones People

Every church has four different kinds of people:

The **wishbones**, who spend their time wishing for success instead of working for it.

The **jawbones**, who talk about success but do very little else.

The **knucklebones**, who knock everything that everyone else is doing.

The **backbones**, who get under the load and get the job done.

Thank God for these people! Pray that the Lord will increase the number of "backbones people" in our church.

Working Together

A man grabbed the other end of a piano when he noticed a storekeeper trying to get it through the door of his store. They struggled for about fifteen minutes, unable to budge the heavy object. Finally the store owner puffed, "I don't think we'll ever get this thing out of the store."

"Get it out!" the man wailed. "I thought we were trying to get it in!"

Church members often waste valuable time and energy working against each other instead of working together. Now is the time for everyone to grab the piano and start pushing in the same direction!

What a Great Idea!

Here's a great idea: Let's divide our church membership into small groups of about ten to twelve people per group.

These groups would meet regularly, even weekly. Each member of a group would know the others personally. There would be times of sharing when any member of the group could open his or her heart to the others.

In times of need, members of the group could minister to one another. Of course, the group could regularly include others—outsiders who are enlisted as new members of the group. This system of enlistment would actually be a great way to reach and evangelize those people who would never come to a worship service of the church.

We could call these groups Sunday school classes. What a great way this would be to grow a church, to minister to our own members, and to reach new people for Christ and church membership!

The Things that Unite the Church

A Savior we can all serve.
A Book we can all understand.
A race we can all run.
A battle we can all win.
A faith we can all keep.
A work we can all do.
A gospel we can all obey.

Needed: Ordinary Christians

General Dwight D. Eisenhower once rebuked an officer for referring to a soldier as "just a private." He reminded the officer that the army could function better without its generals than it could without its foot soldiers. "If this war is won," Ike declared, "it will be won by privates."

In the same way, the common, ordinary, one-talent Christians are the very backbone of the church. We have our great evangelists, our large churches led by dynamic pastors, and our wealthy Christian businessmen who are able to finance big projects that attract a lot of attention. But if the work of the Lord is to be done—if the gospel is to be taken to the lost—it will be the "ordinary" Christians who will accomplish this great work.

One Person Does Count

When you are tempted to believe that your absence from church doesn't matter, consider these facts about the power of a single vote:

In 1654, one vote gave Oliver Cromwell control of England.

In 1845, one vote brought Texas into the Union.

In 1868, one vote saved President Andrew Johnson from impeachment.

In 1876, one vote gave Rutherford B. Hayes the Presidency of the United States.

In 1960, Richard Nixon lost the Presidential election and John F. Kennedy won it by less than one vote per precinct in the United States.

Your presence at church does matter. We'll see you there on the next Lord's Day.

Consumer or Contributor?

Church members come in two basic types: consumers and contributors.

The consumer church member is one whose view of the church centers around what he or she receives. "What have you done for me lately?" is the consumer's attitude. But a contributor church member asks, "What can I do?" The contributor understands that the Christian calling is to service and invests talents, time, and energy in the work of God's kingdom.

Are you a consumer or a contributor? Pray that God will give you a contributor attitude toward his church and the living Savior whom we serve.

What the Church Is Not

The church is
not a place but a people;
not a fold but a flock;
not a sacred building but a
    believing assembly.
The church consists of those
    who pray,
not where they pray.
A structure of bricks
can no more be a church
than clothes can be the
    person
who wears them.

2

Discipleship and Christian Influence

Can We Genuinely Pray the Lord's Prayer?

We cannot pray

"our Father" if we do not have a personal relationship with God.

"who art in heaven" if our interest is in earthly things.

"hallowed be thy name" unless we use God's name with reverence and respect.

"thy kingdom come" if we are not willing to accept God's reign in our lives.

"thy will be done on earth as it is in heaven" unless we give ourselves to God's service.

"give us this day our daily bread" if we ignore the needs of others.

"forgive us our trespasses" if we harbor grudges and hard feelings against others.

"deliver us from evil" if we are not prepared to use the weapon of prayer in resisting the temptations of Satan.

"thine is the kingdom, the power, and the glory forever" if we do not give God the highest priority in our lives.

Not Enough Action

One of our problems as Christians is too many rehearsals and not enough performance. Week after week we assemble to hear preachers and Bible teachers tell about what Jesus and the early Christians did. But we are seldom challenged to put these teachings into practice during the week.

We do not need to rehearse over and over again what has been done in the long ago. We need to get involved in the work which God is doing in the world today.

A Christian Tune-up

1. Adjust your lights so others may see your good works.
2. Set your timing to be in church on time.
3. Adjust the brakes on your tongue so you may always speak well of others.
4. Align your direction to follow the straight and narrow path of God's will.
5. Attune your mind to think on pure and holy things.
6. Anti-freeze your heart; be fervent and zealous in the Lord's service.
7. Lubricate your spirit with the oil of joy and gladness.

Action and Reaction

Take a piece of wax, a morsel of meat, a handful of sand, a pinch of clay, and some wood shavings and put them on a fire. The wax melts; the meat fries; the sand dries up; the clay hardens; the shavings blaze. Although they are subjected to the same fire, each of the objects reacts in a different way.

This is a dramatic reminder of how individuals also react differently to the same circumstances. Subjected to hardship and despair, one person grows stronger, while others weaken or wither away.

One person hears the Word of God and is made better. Others hear the same message and grow angry and rebellious. Let us take heed how we respond to the actions of God in our lives.

My Influence

My life shall touch a dozen lives
Before this day is done;
Leave countless marks for good or ill,
Ere sets the evening sun.

So this the wish I always wish,
The prayer I ever pray;
"Lord, may my life help other lives
It touches by the way."
—Author unknown

Living for Others

Lord, help us live from day to
    day
In such a self-forgetful way
That even when we kneel to
    pray
Our prayer shall be for others.

Others, Lord, yes, others—
Let this our motto be;
Help us to live for others,
That we may live like thee.
    —Author unknown

Do It Now

Do it now—the good you
    can—
True to God and fellowman.
One more day may be too
    late—
Never should we hesitate.

If you have a fragrant flower,
Cheer someone this very
    hour—
Flowers laid upon a tomb
Quickly fade and lose their
    bloom.

If you utter earnest prayer
For a soul with griefs to bear,
God will help both you and
    him
When the way seems rough
    and dim.

In this world of sin and woe,
We the love of God must show.
Do it now if but a smile,
Helping others all the while.
    —Author unknown

The Danger of Drifting

Every boat owner realizes that nothing is easier than drifting. All one has to do is sit back and relax and let the boat go. One may not even be aware he or she is drifting until it is too late and the boat is on the rocks.

Christians also face the temptation of resting on the oars and drifting along in the Christian life. If you are drifting, awaken to the danger now, then grab the oars and pull. Your active concern is essential as you seek to lead the unsaved to find Christ and his will for their lives.

The Ten Commandments Restated

Above all else love God alone;
Bow down to neither wood nor stone.
God's name refuse to take in vain;
The Sabbath rest with care maintain.
Respect your parents all your days;
Hold sacred human life always.
Be loyal to your chosen mate;
Steal nothing, neither small nor great.
Report with truth your neighbor's deed;
And rid your mind of selfish greed.
—Author unknown

Giving the Very Best

If you should invite guests to a meal in your home, you wouldn't warm up leftovers and serve them on paper plates in front of the television. No, you would probably prepare a special meal, use your best china, and spend some quality time with your guests. You would offer them your very best.

In the same way, we should offer the very best to Jesus rather than give him the leftovers of our lives. We bring honor to our Savior when we give him the best of our time, talents, and treasures.

Ten Commandments
for Church Leaders

You shall accept your place of service enthusiastically, believing that God has called you to this task.

You shall do your very best, even when the results are disappointing.

You shall seek to learn your job so you can do it well. You shall be faithful to the worship services of your church.

You shall study the Word of God and spend time in prayer each day.

You shall pray for those who are not Christians and seek to lead them to Christ.

You shall speak well of your church and joyfully lead others to do likewise.

You shall work with the entire program of your church and cooperate with the pastor and staff as well as other leaders.

You shall follow God's plan of Christian stewardship and set an example for others.

You shall seek God's leadership in all matters and follow his will above all else.

3

Evangelism, Visitation, Witnessing

The Wonder of Salvation

The world is full of wonders. Take water, for example. This common substance is made up of hydrogen and oxygen, both of which are flammable by themselves. But unite hydrogen and oxygen into water, and you can put out a fire with it. What a wonder!

Salvation is also a wonder. How God can transform a hopeless sinner into a respectable person is perhaps the greatest wonder of all. Just think: by witnessing to others we can have an important part in one of the wonders of the universe. God will honor our efforts if we will serve as His faithful witnesses.

How Many Times to Visit?

Visit once—and you are fulfilling an obligation.

Visit twice—and you are showing real interest.

Visit three times—and you are demonstrating a real concern for the person.

Visit a fourth time—and you are showing determination.

Visit until you enlist and win the prospect—and you are modeling the love of Christ.

It's Your Move

The moving van presents a great opportunity for you to bear your witness as a Christian. When a new family moves into your community, you can render service in these ways:

1. Get acquainted with the newcomers as soon as possible.
2. Extend warm and courteous friendship.
3. Demonstrate an enthusiasm for your church.
4. Introduce these new neighbors to your friends.
5. Inform them about your church's activities which may be of interest to them.
6. Invite them to attend church with you.
7. Let the church office know so a follow-up visit can be made.

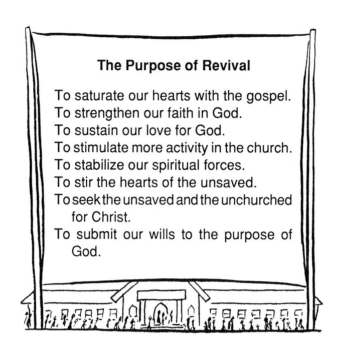

The Purpose of Revival

To saturate our hearts with the gospel.
To strengthen our faith in God.
To sustain our love for God.
To stimulate more activity in the church.
To stabilize our spiritual forces.
To stir the hearts of the unsaved.
To seek the unsaved and the unchurched for Christ.
To submit our wills to the purpose of God.

NOTHING BEATS A PERSONAL VISIT

The Centrality of Visitation

If I advertise in the newspaper and on billboards but do not visit, I become as sounding brass and a tinkling cymbal.

If I have the gift of praying for the lost and understand Daniel and Revelation but do not visit, my church will not grow.

If I take food baskets to the poor and sacrifice my body in church meetings all week long but do not visit, it profiteth me nothing.

Visitation never fails. And now abide letters, phone calls, and visitation—but the greatest of these is visitation.

Seek the People

Any church that wants to win people to Christ must find a way to be where the unsaved multitudes are. These people are not in the church building. They don't come to church; they must be brought. They will not seek; they must be sought. It is our responsibility as Christians to go where these people are and to confront them with the claims of Christ, bringing them under the shelter of his love and salvation.

Definitions of Missions

M is for God's **Mercy** that allows us to live;

I is for **Inspiration** we Christians should give;

S is for **Seeking** for souls that are lost;

S is for the **Savior** who paid the cost;

I is for our **Influence** that portrays what we are;

O is for **Others** who call us from afar;

N is for the **Need** of Christ in every nation;

S is for **Sending** them the story of salvation.

—Author unknown

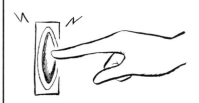

The Power of Personal Visitation

- Would you like to grow as a Christian?

  Personal visitation will do the job.
- Do you want to see our church grow?

  Visitation will do the job.
- Do you want to see lost people won to Christ?

  Visitation will do the job.
- Would you like to see inactive church members become active?

  Visitation will do the job.

Personal visitation is the answer to many needs of our church. Make a commitment today to begin visiting people.

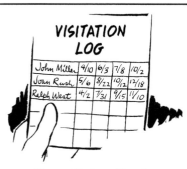

VISITATION LOG

John Miller	4/10	6/3	7/8	10/2
Joan Rush	5/6	8/22	10/12	12/18
Ralph West	4/2	7/31	9/15	11/10

Keep Going Back

In the business world, successful sales people are those who keep going back:

- 48 percent of the sales people quit after only one call.
- 25 percent quit after two.
- 15 percent quit after three.
- The remaining 12 percent of the sales people keep on calling, and these do 80 percent of the business.

Christians should go beyond the sales people of the business world in our attempts to win others. The way to build a great church is to keep going back.

Christ in You

There is but one successful plan
By which to win your fellowman—
Have you a neighbor old or new?
Just let that one see Christ in you.

The church that hopes to win the lost
Must pay the one unchanging cost—
She must compel the world to see
In her the Christ of Calvary.

—Author unknown

4

Inspiration for Daily Living

THE RACE OF LIFE STARTING LINE

How to Win

There is no easy path to glory;
　There is no rosy road to
　　fame;
Life, however we may view it,
　Is no simple parlor game.

No, its prizes call for fighting,
　For endurance and for grit,
For a rugged disposition,
　And a "don't-know-when-
　　to-quit."

You must take a blow or give
　one;
　You must risk and you must
　　lose
And expect that in the struggle,
　You will suffer and be
　　bruised.

But you mustn't wince or
　falter
　If a fight you once begin;
Be a man and face the battle—
　That's the only way to win.
　　　　　　　　—Author unknown

Our Best Friends

May we never take for granted
　All the folks we know the
　　best;
They are oft the very people
　By whose lives we're truly
　　blessed.
　　　　　　　　—Author unknown

The Lamp of Love

Love in a home is like a lamp
Around whose steady glow
The children gather safe and
warm
    Though storms outside
may blow.

And in the shadowy years to
come,
    The children long since
grown
Will light love's lamps in other
homes
For children of their own.
          —Barbara Dolliver

Wanted: Humble Shepherds

A cartoon pictured the angry parents of a boy who had been selected to play not the lead role but the part of a shepherd in the school's annual Christmas pageant. "But somebody has to be a humble shepherd," the boy's teacher retorted.

Like these parents, too many of us relish the starring role. We want to be front and center—the key player in the entire production. But God needs humble shepherds as well as stars. Nothing we do in his service should be looked on as insignificant or unimportant.

Lessons from a Watermelon Seed

It would take thousands of watermelon seeds to weigh a pound. Yet when one single seed is planted and nurtured under the right conditions, it can produce several watermelons that weigh forty or fifty pounds each. Such are the wonders of nature—and the miracle-working God who is the master force behind nature's grand design.

Just as a watermelon seed multiplies itself by several thousand times, God can make of us far more than we are if we will let him work his miracles in our lives.

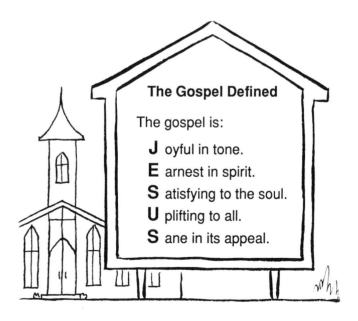

The Gospel Defined

The gospel is:

J oyful in tone.
E arnest in spirit.
S atisfying to the soul.
U plifting to all.
S ane in its appeal.

Stumbling Block or Stepping-Stone?

Isn't it strange that princes
   and kings
And clowns that caper in saw-
   dust rings
And common people like you
   and me
Are builders for eternity?

Each is given a bag of tools,
A shapeless mass, and a book
   of rules;
And each must make, 'ere life
   has flown,
A stumbling block or a
   stepping-stone.

—R. L. Sharpe

Spendthrifts in Love

Christians should be spendthrifts in love. Love is the one treasure that actually multiplies as we give it away. The more we take from it, the bigger it grows.

Give love away; splash it generously on others; empty your pockets; shake the basket; turn the glass upside down—and tomorrow you will have more than ever.

61

A Big Person

I wish I were:

BIG ENOUGH to honestly admit all my shortcomings;

BROAD ENOUGH to accept flattery without becoming vain;

TALL ENOUGH to tower above deceit;

STRONG ENOUGH to treasure love;

BRAVE ENOUGH to welcome criticism;

COMPASSIONATE ENOUGH to understand human frailties;

WISE ENOUGH to stand by my friends;

HUMAN ENOUGH to be thoughtful of my neighbor;

RIGHTEOUS ENOUGH to be devoted to the laws of God.

—Author unknown

A Tea Party for Me

Before we can minister to other people, we have to give ourselves. Perhaps too many of us have the selfish attitude reflected in this poem:

I had a little tea party
This afternoon at three.
'Twas very small—
Three guests in all—
Just I, myself, and me.

Myself ate all the sandwiches,
While I drank up the tea;
'Twas also I who ate the pie
And passed the cake to me.

People all wrapped up in themselves cannot share themselves with other people. Only Christ can deliver us from our selfishness and open our eyes to the needs of others.

My Song to Sing

He placed me in a little cage
    Away from gardens fair;
But I must sing the sweetest
        song
    Because he placed me
        there.

Not beat my wings against
        the gate,
    If it's my maker's will,
But raise my voice to heaven's
        gate
    And sing the louder still.
    —Author unknown

Climbing the Mountain

The path is winding, skies are
        gray,
    The mountainside is steep;
How much farther must I travel
    Before I rest and sleep?

But I shall scale the lofty height
    For I am not alone;
My Lord has walked this path
        before—
    The way to him is known.

He leads me up the narrow
        way
    As shepherds lead their
        sheep;
He guides me through the
        darkening gloom
    And over rocky steeps.

When I pass through the last
        dark cloud
    And reach the mountain
        crest,
The long, hard climb will be
        forgotten—
    Then God and I will rest.
    —Helen Hazel

5

Seasonal and Christian Year

Christmas Reminders

May Christmas

gifts remind you of God's greatest gift, His only begotten Son.

candles remind you of Him who is the "Light of the world."

trees remind you of another tree upon which He died for you.

cheer remind you of Him who said, "Be of good cheer."

bells remind you of the glorious proclamation of His birth.

carols remind you of the song the angels sang, "Glory to God in the highest."

season remind you in every way of Jesus Christ your King.

Ten Commandments for Christmas

1. Thou shalt not leave Christ out of Christmas.
2. Thou shalt not value thy gifts by their costs.
3. Thou shalt give thyself with thy gifts.
4. Thou shalt not let Santa Claus take the place of Jesus Christ.
5. Thou shalt spend sensibly and responsibly.
6. Thou shalt not neglect the church.
7. Thou shalt not forget the needy.
8. Thou shalt experience Christmas as a little child.
9. Thou shalt prepare yourself spiritually for Christmas.
10. Thou shalt give to missions.

If you try to keep these ten commandments this Christmas, you will experience the true joy and love that the Christ of Christmas offers.

God's Gift upon a Tree

The first great Christmas gift
    to men
  Was hung upon a tree;
It was not by a fireside,
  Where only those could see

Who were near to kin or
  friendship
  And gifts exchanged would
  be,
But out upon a mountain side
  For all the world to see.
        —Author unknown

Not a Martyr

'Twas not a martyr's death he
  died,
  The Christ of Calvary,
It was a willing sacrifice
  He made for you, for me.

He could have summoned
  angel hosts
  The wicked hands to stay,
But well he knew salvation's
  plan
  Was founded on that day!

Nay! Not a martyr, but instead
  A sacrifice for me—
He died the death of Calvary's
  cross
  To set a lost world free.
        —Georgia B. Adams

Meet My Dad

I wish you could meet my Dad;
　He's really quite a guy!
I wouldn't trade with anyone,
　And here's the reason why:

Whenever I have problems,
　Doubts, or questions, too,
We talk them over—Dad
　and I—
And find what's best to do.

He helps me practice base-
　ball,
　And gives me useful tips;
And even lets me go along
　When he takes fishing trips!

Then, too, my Dad's a Chris-
　tian;
　We often kneel and pray;
He helps me live as Jesus
　taught.
Yes sir, my Dad's O.K.
　　　—Author unknown

Portrait of a Dad

God took the strength of a
　mountain,
　The majesty of a tree,
The warmth of the summer
　sunshine,
　The calm of a quiet sea.

The generous soul of nature,
　The comforting arms of
　night,
The wisdom of the ages,
　The power of an eagle's
　flight.

The joy of a summer morning,
　The faith of a mustard seed,
The patience of eternity,
　The depth of a family's
　need.

God combined these quali-
　ties,
　And with nothing more to
　add,
He knew his masterpiece was
　complete—
　And so he called it Dad.
　　　—Herbert Farnham

A Father's Example

There are little eyes upon you,
    And they're watching night and day;
There are little ears that listen
    To every word you say.

There are little hands all eager
    To do the things you do;
And a little boy who's dreaming
    Of the day he'll be like you.

You're the little fellow's idol,
    You're the wisest of the wise;
In his little mind, about you
    No suspicions ever rise.

He believes in you devoutly,
    Holds that all you say and do
He will say and do in your way
    When he's grown up just like you.

There's a wide-eyed little fellow
    Who believes you're always right;
And his ears are always open
    As he watches day and night.

You are setting an example
    Every day in all you do,
For the little boy who's waiting
    To grow up to be like you.
             —Edgar A. Guest

A Mother's Secret

Someone asked a mother whose children had turned out well how she had prepared them for usefulness and Christian living.

"When I bathed my children," she replied, "I prayed they might be cleansed by the precious blood of Christ.

"When I helped them get dressed for the day, I prayed they might be clothed in the robe of God's righteousness.

"When I prepared a meal, I prayed they might be fed with the Bread of Life.

"When I saw them off to school, I prayed their faith might grow just as strong as their bodies and minds.

"When I put them to bed at night, I prayed they might be safe in the everlasting arms of our Savior."

A Mother's Reward

I do not ask that you repay
    The hours of toil and pain;
The sacrifice of youth and
    strength
    Shall not have been in vain.

I do not ask for gratitude
    But only this, my child,
That you shall live your life so
    well
    My gifts be not defiled.

The nights I watched beside
    your crib,
    The years of love and care
Will amply be repaid if once
    I see you standing there;

An upright and an honest soul
    On whom success has
    smiled,
That I may say with humble
    pride—
    "That is my child!"
        —Freeman Lathrop

The Uncrowned Queen

When God would save a world from sin,
He chose with mothers to begin;
And, through a virgin mother birth,
To bring good will to men on earth.

When Christ the way of life would tell,
A woman listened by a well;
When he was tired and needed rest,
Two women honored Him as guest;
He caused a maid to walk again,
And raised a widow's son at Nain.

A mother's love will stand by you,
When other friends have proved untrue;
She'll round your bed her vigil keep,
While other eyes are closed in sleep;
She'll cleave to you till life shall end
And be your dearest friend.

Our mothers steer the ship of state;
'Tis they who make the nation great.
Our nation will be bad or good,
According to its motherhood.
And back of all great men is seen,
The image of an uncrowned queen.

—Author unknown

Midyear Resolutions Review

You've probably forgotten the resolutions you made at the beginning of this year. Here are a few you might consider as a midyear resolutions review. They're guaranteed to make you a better person, no matter when you observe them:

Keep me from the habit of thinking I must say something on every subject on every occasion.

Release me of the burden of trying to straighten out everybody's affairs.

Make me thoughtful but not moody; helpful but not bossy.

Keep my mind free of the recital of endless details. Give me wings to get to the point.

Seal my lips on my aches and pains. They are increasing, and my love of hearing them is becoming sweeter as the years go by.

I ask not for improved memory but a growing humility when my memory seems to clash with the memory of others.

Teach me the glorious lesson that, occasionally, I may be mistaken.

Give me the ability to see good things in unexpected places and talents in unexpected people.

If I Had Last Year to Live Over Again

If I had last year to live over, I would pay more attention to people. I would try to express the warmth and affection that I feel for them. I would send a note of good wishes when good things happened in their lives.

I wouldn't be satisfied to send a routine greeting on holidays. I would write a personal note. I would set up a file on a few of my closest friends to remind me to write a word of encouragement to them on their birthday. I would be more careful to answer every personal letter promptly and to keep the channels of communication open.

Since last year can't be recalled, I resolve to do these things in the new year ahead.

Resolutions for the New Year

A little less impatience with
  those we deem too slow;
A little less arrogance because
  of all we know;
A little more humility, seeing
  our worth is slight . . .
We are such trivial candles
  compared to stars at night!

A little more forgiving and
  swifter to be kind;
A little more desirous the word
  of praise to find,
The word of praise to utter
  and make a heart rejoice;
A little bit more careful to speak
  with gentle voice.

A little more true eagerness to
  understand each other;
A little more high courage to
  help a ship-wrecked
  brother;
A little more real striving for
  each task that must be
  done;
These be our resolutions . . .
  and God help everyone!
—Author unknown

Our Wish for You
Next Year

During the year ahead, may you have:

Enough **happiness** to keep you sweet;
Enough **trials** to keep you strong;
Enough **sorrow** to keep you human;
Enough **hope** to keep you happy;
Enough **failure** to keep you humble;
Enough **success** to keep you eager;
Enough **friends** to give you comfort;
Enough **faith** and **courage** in yourself, your work, and your country to banish your depression;
Enough **wealth** to meet your needs;
Enough **determination** to make each day a better day than yesterday.

—E. M. Garrett

Our Lives as
Thanksgiving

Let our lives be our thanksgiving
To our Father up above;
Let us worship him with kindness;
Let us praise him with our love.

Let us honor him with virtue;
Let good deeds become our prayer;
Let our lives be our thanksgiving
For the bounty that we share.

—Author unknown

A Thanksgiving Prayer

We thank thee, God, for blessings—
  The big ones and the small—
Thy tender love and mercy
  That guards and keeps us all.

The fresh awakening of joy
  That comes with morning light,
Sunlit hours to fill the day
  And restful sleep at night.

The hope, the beauty, and the love
  That brighten each day's living—
We praise thee, and our hearts are filled
  With joy, and with thanksgiving.

The pride that's found in work well done,
  The love of those who care,
The peace of mind, the sweet content
  That comes with quiet prayer.
  —Author unknown

The Asset of Gratitude

People reckon up their goods—so much in bonds, so much in stocks, so much in notes, so much in personal property, so much in real estate. In taking account of our possessions, do we ever take into consideration the asset of a thankful heart? Probably not. And yet there is no greater wealth in itself, and no greater producing agent of wealth than the faculty of gratitude.

Contentment is a personal feast. The richest man in the world can use no more than enough for his wants. If you have the same, you are as rich as he is.

A Different Kind
of Thanksgiving

We thank thee, Father, for the care
   That did not come to try us,
The burden that we did not bear,
   The trouble that passed by us.

The task we did not fail to do,
   The hurt we did not cherish,
The friend who did not prove untrue,
   The joy that did not perish.

We thank thee for the blinding storm
   That did not lose its swelling,
And for the sudden blight of harm
   That came not near our dwelling.

We thank thee for the dart unsped,
   The bitter word unspoken,
The grave unmade, the tear unshed,
   The heart-tie still unbroken.
                    —Author unknown

6

Sentence Sermons

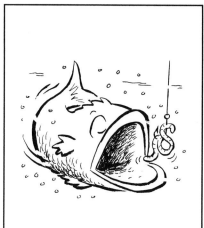

Don't Take the Bait

Even a fish would stay out of trouble if it kept its mouth shut.

The Great Room

The largest room in the world is the room for improvement.

A Productive Sitter

A hen is the only creature that can sit around and still be a producer.

Caution: Words Forming

Be careful of your thoughts; they could break into words at any time.

Pressure's Product

A diamond is a piece of coal that made good under pressure.

Face the Wind

Don't be afraid of opposition; a kite rises against the wind, not with it.

Clean Living

So live that you would not hesitate to sell the family parrot to the town gossip!

The Sounds of Nothing

Why is it that people who know the least always know it the loudest?

Slow Arrival

The best thing about the future is that it arrives only one day at the time.

Interrupted by Life

Life is what happens while you are making other plans.

The Awkward Age

Middle age is that tough time between adolescence and retirement when you have to take care of yourself.

Rare People

Friends are those rare people who ask you how you are and then listen to your reply.

Too Much Learning

The trouble with a lot of people is that they are educated beyond their intelligence.

Creative Writing

The closest most people ever come to reaching their potential is when they write their resumés.

A Powerful One

If you think one person cannot make a difference in the world, consider what one cigar can do in a crowded restaurant!

A Real Shortage

Our nation's number-one energy crisis is Monday morning.

Busybodies

Idle gossip keeps some people very busy.

Lightning Fast

A lie can travel half way around the world while the truth is putting on its shoes.

When Less Means More

As a person grows wiser, he talks less and says more.

Knowing Your Limits

One big part of being smart is knowing what you are dumb at.

7

Miscellaneous

Not Enough

He knew the Book from A to Z,
His mind had mastered
every part;
A fine achievement—but alas!
It never got into his heart.

—Author unknown

Jesus Is Able

He is able to save (Heb. 7:25).
He is able to keep you from
falling (Jude 24).
He is able to help those who
are tempted (1 Cor. 10:13).
He is able to do for us more
than we ask or think (Eph.
3:20).
He is able to make all grace
abound (2 Cor. 9:8).

Cirrhosis of the Giver

The strange disease known as cirrhosis of the giver was first noted during New Testament times in a couple known as Ananias and Sapphira (see Acts 5:1–11). This malady is an acute condition that renders victim's hands immobile when they are called on to move them to wallets or purses, and from there to offering plates.

Most churches have dozens of members who suffer from this disease. The only hope for these people is to get their lives in tune with God's will. He can cure cirrhosis of the giver and turn his people into generous, joyful givers and faithful financial supporters of the church.

Safe Giving

A farmer boasted to his pastor that he would give half of everything he owned to God.

"That's good," his pastor replied. "If you had thirty pigs, would you give fifteen to the Lord?"

"Of course I would."

"If you had ten, would you give five?"

"You know I would."

"Fine," said his pastor. "If you had two pigs, would you give one to the Lord?"

"Now hold on, pastor," the farmer protested. "You know I have two pigs."

How easy it is to promise to share what we don't have with the Lord. But the real test of Christian stewardship is to give a share of those resources with which God has already blessed our lives.

Wind and Thunder

An Indian attended a worship service where he heard a loud, thunderous sermon with little substance. Someone asked him how he liked the sermon.

"High wind, big thunder, no rain!" he replied.

The Carpenter of Galilee

The carpenter of Galilee
　　Comes down the street again,
In every land, in every age,
　　He still is calling men.

On any day we hear him knock—
　　He goes from door to door—
Are any workmen out of work?
　　The carpenter needs more.
　　　　　　—Hilda W. Smith

Definition of a Christian Family

A Christian family is one in which parents live the Christian life and practice the presence of God so their children come to accept God as the greatest reality of life.

A Christian family is one in which each member is accepted and respected as a person of sacred worth.

A Christian family is one that seeks to bring every member into the Christian way of living.

A Christian family is one that accepts the responsibility of worship and Christian instruction in order to develop the spiritual life of each person.

A Christian family is one that shows its faith in God, observes daily prayer, and offers thanks to God at mealtimes.

A Christian family is one that is committed to Christian behavior in the family, community, and world.